KINGDOMLAND

RACHAEL ALLEN

# Kingdomland

FABER & FABER

First published in 2019
by Faber & Faber Ltd
Bloomsbury House
74–77 Great Russell Street
London WC1B 3DA

Typeset by Hamish Ironside
Printed in England by TJ International Ltd, Padstow, Cornwall

A CIP record for this book is available from the British Library

ISBN 978-0-571-34111-5

MIX
Paper from
responsible sources
FSC® C013056

4 6 8 10 9 7 5

# Contents

# Acknowledgements

This book is for my family.

'Landscape for a Dead Woman' is written in memory. The title is inspired by Carolyn Steedman's *Landscape for a Good Woman*. The poem opens with a quotation from 'Later' by Rae Armantrout.

'Prawns of Joe' is written after Selima Hill's 'Prawns de Jo'.

A number of these poems are written in response to or in collaboration with visual artworks by Guy Gormley, Marie Jacotey, Vera Iliatova, Anna Mahler and JocJonJosch. I am grateful to these artists for their work.

Thank you to the editors of *Ambit*, *Art Licks*, *Chicago Review*, *LEAF!*, *Magma*, *Poetry*, *Poetry London*, *Poetry Review*, *The Rialto*, *Test Centre*, *The Verb* and *The Wolf*, where some of these poems first appeared.

Thank you to Guy Robertson and Eva LeWitt at the Mahler & LeWitt Studios, and Cathy Rozel Farnworth at the Roger and Laura Farnworth Poetry and Art Residency in Cornwall.

Thank you to Matthew Hollis and Lavinia Singer for their editorial guidance.

Thank you to Sam Buchan-Watts, Sophie Collins, Lukus Roberts, Andrew Parkes, John Wedgwood Clarke, Harriet Moore, Fiona Benson, Jess Chandler, Hannah Barry, Jack Underwood, Sam Riviere, Nuar Alsadir, Patrick Mackie, Ann Gray and David Woolley for your guidance and help with these poems.

# KINGDOMLAND

Watch the forest burn
with granular heat.

A girl, large-eyed
pressure in a ditch

grips to a dank and
disordered root system

no tongue
flavoured camo

bathing in the black
and emergent pool.

See the trees on fire
char simultaneously

as the girl floats up
to the billowing ceiling.

# Promenade

Openly wanting something
like the opened-up lungs of a singer.
I walk by the carriage of the sea
and the vinegar wind assaults.
Is this an age of promise? I blush
to want. If I were walking around
with you, arm in arm, along some
iron promenade, you could fill me up
with chocolate, you could push back
my cuticles with want. I'll just lie down,
my ribs opened up in the old town square
and let the pigs root through my chest.

# Kingdomland

The dark village sits on the crooked hill.
There is a plot of impassable paths towards it,
impassable paths overcome with bees,
the stigma that bees bring.
There is a bottle neck at the base of the hive.
There is an impassable knowledge that your eyebrows bring.
Beside the poor library and the wicker-man,
there's a man who sells peacock feathers on the roundabout,
they scream all night from where they are plucked.
The village is slanted, full of tragedies with slate.

I am walking towards a level crossing,
while someone I love is jogging into the darkness.
*Come away from there*, I am yelling,
while the black dog rolls in the twilit yard.
Small white socks bob into the dark like teeth in the mouth
of a laughing man, who walks backwards into night,
throwing drinks into the air
like a superstitious wife throws salt.
We all have our share of certainties.
The glass and salt my petulant daughter,
glass and salt my crooked pathway; impassable glass and salt.

## Prawns of Joe

When I had a husband I found it hard to breathe.
I was up early, he'd get home late
to rub the baby, we took it in turns.
He left, and if someone knocked for him
now at the door
I would not let him go to them.
In among all the crying, I see
a burning child on the stove.
The same one as before?
The curtains are full of soot. Well quickly,
we need to escape. Well surely.
No, I watch her burn.

What is it I love about the sound of dogs barking
as smoke rises out the window?
What a complete noise, like a pile of hands clapping.
Another body found burned in the oval,
purple and mystical,
and all around her
peppery crisps in the shape of a heart.

There's a woman over the road
who moved in when he left.
She has a black little finger
and has been watching me for days.
Her shadow is that of a man's in the right light.
Sometimes she's right outside the window
sometimes I think she's in the house
in the cupboard under the sink
or behind the shower curtain.

I hold her name like grit between my teeth
turning cartwheels by the edge of the stream.
The air is touchy, fibreglass,
summer streams through the trees like a long blonde hair.
I want to grab all the things that make me ashamed
and throw them from the bridge
like how I don't like the sun at the end of the day,
eating cold cream cake on the dimming porch
in the yellow breeze, lonely,
just thinking up these stories.
So I fling my fork into the bark like a stroppy dictator,
it makes that cartoon stuck-in-wood noise.
I am stuck in the middle of the month (again).
I would like to have some time on my hands
something like a stain.
Happy Birthday floats up to my window
followed by your name, your purple name.

## Monstrous Horses

I jumped I lit the noose
on fire, a great lemon
in place of my heart, a start.
I am falling without help
down a steep white cliff
saluting magpies in hope.
I pass two horses stood end to end
making one monstrous double horse.
Off in the distance
I notice with a start
a horizon line of sons
hammering chalk.
The forest beneath them is so green
it is an optical illusion
mounted on foam.

## Lunatic Urbaine

The man who loved me
pushed me to the ground
in a pool of white plants.
When we tell you to stop,
we whispered, you stop,
and the trees are above us
knitting out the sky.
There's nothing like a man
to serve you pain deep-seared
on a silver dish that rings
when you flick it, your table
gilded and festooned
with international meats,
cured and crusted, each
demanding its own sauce.
I ask to be taken home
but of course I am home,
so I turn my attention elsewhere.

# Volcano

A bleak and ferrous opening in the sky
a wound the kind that rots to black
rumbling apart, a doctored element of cloud.

Beneath that, a geography observed from a ship,
an old great state at the base of an eruption
where only girls lived, carbuncled in dust,
caught mid-play and mid-menses, long arms
chastising or rubbing filth on themselves, arched
over desks and on the swings, illicitly being.

## Simple Men

Under-lit like a driveway, haunted and beech-lined,
obtuse crevices, attention-seeking,
damaged with names they're unforgivably given.
Deep, apoplectic Daniel, who hides in the wood
sad about a failing relationship with his mother.
For a laugh I told him he was adopted,
brother Daniel, and he beat me to a pulp.

The face of a girl fills up with blood
when she is touched too much
and commits herself to rage.
What is she watching come in over the shore
from the corner of her eye
as she sulks lazily by the large bay window?
A haunted old body, the one she'll inhabit
that drags up and down the coast.

Nights of Poor Sleep

*Dear Former Love,*

*Meeting you in the first place was great though*


I am the girl with chapped cheeks and blue bow
with my breasts taped down
dancing silently on my father's lap
of course I wake with a start in the
new bedroom
painted blue
in a cacophonous pool of blood

the moon sways over me whitely
too quickly
bordered by trees
in the ghost town where I live

strange feelings overcame me when he left
like the cracking old image of a wave framing a lighthouse
like an octopus crawling on land

he was a god in his blood thirst
looking out of the window, a pre-ghost
I know the look of someone newly murdered
the moon's trailing over me too quickly

outside the window, trees darkly mask the sky
the sky the thatched colour of jeans
evening coming down like hair snipped over shoulders
everything in place for our inflatable dinner party
we sat courteously as adults, haloed by stained glass

efforts to understand me were lost
like music reverberating under water or a hammock
pinged at one end
my safe word couldn't reach him with his head at my tail
spanking me pinkly into the crawl space
I wore rose gold rings to impress him
(she got there first)
this was outside my character

*Rodeo fun on a Sunday*


In the living room is a man who loves me more than the
     last man
who made me feel like I was falling from a cliff
and if it feels like you're falling from a cliff
you just might be

awful feeling when the sun begins to thinly shine at dawn
as in the Arctic or on Mars
who knows what the sun's doing there
my eyes don't focus completely
giving everything a crescent edge
so when I look into the pupil of my lover
it has to dilate

don't give up the ghost
I followed him all around Surrey
around the larger parts of an unfamiliar forest
he took me to the cheap parts of Sheen
we made love in a net curtain
it took me hours to lift the pattern from my thigh
it was the only time I wore a blouse
and he blew his nose all over it

suppose just once he tried to impress my father
taking him fishing, pulling up long waders and just striding
     into the lake
until he's actually drowning
why will no one put themselves through that for me?

for my long-suffering father
who perambulates in his head across the table
lowering his glasses
he can smell what they're about to do
like a damn police dog
he drops his head down on his chest

## Morning Defeats

I map a constellation
I am a cucumber
made entirely of water
like my face-down sister
made also entirely of water
we're so full of it
sailors topple off the deck
in wet and dusty mushroom hats
they look like mascots in a doughnut shop
cascading smiling past the portholes
with flags in their pockets
they would have been nice to take home
in my polka-dot bikini
they just can't stop looking
at me

*What a summer we had*


Butter on the wind while
my friends are unprotected
trumpets above and behind the clouds like every painting
   of heaven
hands up who cries themselves to sleep here
at the memory jogged
of one black leaf on the inside of an arm
a smiling face haunting a cloud
I know there is something still between us
why else would you be so cruel?
the cruel way
you stir a tea
the cruel way you sit elsewhere
it's too hard not to touch someone's arm in a way that is
innocent and not innocent
a little squeeze
we use too many materials we don't own
especially to tell each other we feel fondly
things could have been different but not markedly so
tell me on the phone just once something that will feel like
a small match striking at the base of my neck
the immutable drawing together clichéd and true

*You look unwell, my dear*


I make everyone jealous I know
when I saunter into the cafe two streets away
turn left turn left again
when I walk in the door
lipstick on my teeth
a pair of pants hanging around my arm
little smacked-on stain
no one talks when I walk in
and I look everyone in the eye
get some ice cream
anyway I go in there sometimes and just fall to my knees
like life is overwhelming when it's not
everyone looks at me
I'm having problems with my vision, sort of short lines
    of blue
perhaps becoming blinder

*When dawn comes loaded with fear*

The night salesmen
throw themselves against the door
and I am covered in dread
they keep me up all night
they pretend
I am asleep
squeeze pamphlets through the letter box
and bellow through the cat flap
my beautiful friend
mottled torso
framed on the wall
stuck up with tape
I can't take my eyes off him
I reach
a peak with the night salesmen
fling open the door
and grab one by the throat in a frenzy
he is blind
I spit in his blind eye
it is an affectation
like my own blindness

*No last kiss*


Lilac keys to the shared front door
little lilac crystal on the shared keyring
lilac leaves of my drooping spider plant
moulting on the bath mat
so it looks like I've had my purple period

I wonder which one I might speak to first
boys in the forest, police dog dad
bag-of-sticks body wrapped in plastic in the back garden
I lie to basically everyone

I played a ham-fisted stick-in-the-mud
let him stick it where the sun don't shine
played games and played pretending we might want to
pee on each other
let him watch my crocodile tears in the loo
played in the plain yellow wallpaper
while everyone tutted, needed to get on with their day
played in the long-grassed meadow
and it didn't feel as good as I thought it might
played at happiness in a night full of unimaginable grief
and it felt better than I thought it could

outside the window hens click
scuttling around my feet like lizards
losing their legs and growing them back
and changing their names
and losing their spines

*And the face in the mirror, no longer familiar*


The men in my life, yes, come and go
while outside the window insects thrum
there are a mass of clovers
tangling up in something
my cup of bedside water is very still

this is just what happened to me
I suppose it happens to many others
if you wear pink dungarees
at an amiable age

I'm trying to reach you
from my position beetled in this stranger's bedroom
girl legs up towards the familiar cream ceiling
I'm taped up with masking and broken-hearted
in the end he would barely touch me
were I to stay long enough to scrape dark butter
onto toast
mad and thatched
something skinny as the passageway between lines
a concertina of worry
I'd leave them this

Grow up
girl in
silver. No
adult jewellery
no adult
feelings
compromise
is a word
that belongs
in the desert.
I despise
men in
hard hats
entering me
singing as
they do so
as though
they're at the
pulpit. Put
her in the
river. I will
decide where
she ends up
guilty as
ever, filled
up with salt.

# Many Bird Roast

I came in, dandy and present
arguing for a moratorium on meat
of the kind splayed out on the table, legs akimbo
like a fallen-over ice skater skidding on her backside
there are dogs in the outhouse and all over the world
that we do not eat
and one small sparrow in a pigeon in a grouse in a swan
that we will certainly eat
overlooking all the drama, with as many eyes as a spider
that we'll cut in two
and the compacted layers of the various meats
will collapse away dreamily as a rainbow melts down
into the marsh where it came from
slipping meat from the bone
onto a specially designed knife
there's a call out for plates –
I'm the only one with a sense of outcry
someone says, *you weren't like this when it was broiling away*
*smelling like your history, smelling like*
*the deep skin on your knee after playing in the sun all day*
*skinned with good dirt*
*and your under-blood just showing through*
*smelling like warm dry firs after burning and the outdoors*
*after fireworks and Novembers after tea*
*you eat and smell like the rest of us*
*dirty rat under your armpit*
*dirty bird in your stomach*
and birds fell down the chimney with thwacks into buckets
and we got so poor we had to eat them too
strange cockatoos and once a brilliantly lit pure white dove

that we kept in a hutch with a small pot of ink
and when we let it out
it wasn't so much a raven as just a plain black dove
ready to cook, and with superstition, I learnt to.

# Sweet'n Low

A BBQ in the barracks
for a saintly boy
his ears like caravan antennae.
Afternoon weather is
generic, like ice on the
steamy road metaphor,
not the eclipsing
originality of
an elephant.
I am so angry
for the octopus
swallowed in kitsch restaurants.
Quit it,
though I still wear the skin of animals
every day.

# Beef Cubes

hot tight Penny
that girl at school

who put talc on her face
and sausage blush

on her cheeks
was a meat clown

Terry felt through her jean shorts
told everyone she was wet

push him off your lap
we told her, thong showing

brown squares in the pastry bin
as she'd been sick

she was incredibly thin
and kept getting thinner

like when you turn a kind of mirror
till you're flat. Muscle memory

from her panic attacks
kept her off the beach

where the whale cut in half
exudes its yellow fat

and the tourists come
stroked and swollen

on its back, like you
hot tight Penny

its fin a Hot Pocket
people milling as the sun sets

laying down blankets
one beef patty turning on the grill

by the large blue carcass
by the large blue sea

# The Indigo Field

Two bees hang
around a severed horse's head
forgetting that they're supposed to
pollinate
flowers instead of
the roughly opened gland
of a mammal.
Black pennies
with cow faces
down a black well.
You stood no chance
of being born
I tell myself, as the sea
cannibalises.
It manages to forgive itself
every day, without visions
of the baby
making her way towards me
across the indigo field.

# Seer

There she lies aching over enamel,
a blood bath in the city. An animal
hounded, an ingrate up to the gates,
ungracious house guest, keening,
a dog's deep growling on the turn.
The green bank that insists on being
revealed down the insides of legs,
like the muttering stranger
who jumps out from behind a tree.
The white ocean spreads itself
like the badly iced top of a cake
seen through the smeared Plexiglas
of a cheap hotel restaurant.
I grate flesh into garlanded toilet water,
rearrangements of a desiccated sky.
A sound pooled in water, as oil pools
in water, a ghost caught in the layers.

Intestinal scorching, a stomach of shavings.
Being haunted by a baby is worse
than you'd think. I don't want her,
an ingrown ghost, intermittent horror,
the same horror of no stars on a clear night
that means you see nothing in the dark.
The kind of dark you find inside a body.
The kind of darkness you find a body in.
Sick honeysuckle on the air smell
and all around the hotel, rural noises.
The sky is wet with blood and solvent,
sinewy like a fish spine, illuminated
with stars like bone-ends. If you climb
onto the roof and watch this weather
from the weather vane, to hold this
poor memory up, like a sacrifice
to the firmament, you will be exposed.

# Dad the Pig

with a Snickers
in his trough.
I dreamed this poem
knee deep
in silk –
I mean silo.
Slice him up
there's a vacancy
in the sky
and complacency
in the sty.
Who's useful after that
vasectomy anyway?
Someone painted him
in pigeony colours
everyone knows
they're the worst
crayons
(they'd run out
of flesh pencil
well it is the rarest
colour in
the tin).
Ball him up
like an egg
careful of his
front bits
wobbling.
His turkey neck
sack like a

dangling
testicle
stretched down
to the dirt in
blow-job pose
escaped man
fallen to the sand
on his knees
in prayer pose
pinched and dead
puffer fish
on the end of a line
in its last
breath pose.
At night Mam
dreams of taut
hot pigs
bullish and red
with blue veins.
She wears him
calls him
the big holdall
keeps him in the loft
only takes him out
when we go camping.

## Porcine Armour Thyroid

I am a gland, the smooth opal gland
of a pig, who is bubbly with glands
and the glands torn open in this pig's
shorn neck look like droplets of sperm
on the end of your glans. I eat the glands
of pigs for breakfast, and I take a few
in pills each night, slipping down my throat
a smooth oblong, like oysters or snot.
I rub the loose oil glands in my hands
to moisturise, pale mermaid's purses
salted like eyeballs, like lychees, and then
I bathe in some glands, slipping round
each other, the miscreant lump under skin
a gland enlarged with the promise of sickness
grey and portentous, a gland cut open
and placed within another gland creates
a geode of glands, the colour of bad livers
the smell of bad lungs, full of poor white
blood cells, or good white blood cells
or the blood work of a pig, whatever's
farthest, most holy, to the ground.

# Cravendale

Purblind monkey
purblind fatted cow
waiting in the queue for the contract
made on her behalf
low in the muddy sundown
their moans create the dusk
not the other way around
stinking path up to the freezer
further up still from the abattoir
the thin incision on her leg
so she'll kneel before walking
on the plates of her knees
up the old gravel road
a cow in slow and silent
moonlight, grass in her ear
no cow is really a mother
but to milk in the air
or air as milk
or milk in her eye
like a hot blue steam room
holding worlds of fat
mysterious for our benefit
in pictures of the quaintest
traditions cream is tugged
into pails
while in the background
pyres burn on
her low down warm front
puddles on the gravel
cow, eye as a creed

or the look into your eye she makes
a bond, you imagine
moving past you on her knees
caved in from the walk
but laud the pole
that mighty design
like a bolt through the head
there's one still fox
looking up at me
from the field of sheep
as I go by – he's the advert
at the window
as I'm falling straight down

Crying girl
in the canopy
branch held
unstable
a face drawn
pendant-
shaped, from
the bark
marks
how like
a tree is
a woman
crumbling
with age
conversations
inaudible
without a
stethoscope
to the forest
floor and
even then
we whisper.

# The Girls of Situations

History holds the incorrect theories of the sea and how they don't fall off the land, made up by men. Small clouds align. Theories of worship. Women's bodies collect material the way metals accrue in organs. The accumulation of chemical residue, the red bricks of the day in a woman's chest like weights on a diver ungracefully stomping into the lake.

Behind me, a genealogy of red-cheeked maids in maroon-check pinafores. Not a hair out of place, no boarding school narrative, babies shooting from them, straightening beds, nursing while smoking, in labour with rosacea burns, hairs on their breasts wet with the strain. From them I have taken yellow hands and knees, arthritic from kneeling to scrub.

The man he tells you he is not tells you to get an abortion. I live in skirt-behaviours round the social club, where men and cheap beer will spin you till you're sick. Governance is bountiful other than for the young girl who swims out to sea for her reckless behaviour. I make my face white and orange for the jewellery I expect to own. A mimic octopus might be many things but it cannot mimic me.

I stayed with a man after work who kept tarantulas in the loft space. I had on my mint deli uniform and my face was grey. I cut cheese all day long and ham on an industrial slicer. I didn't want to see the bastard black legs of the largest tarantula, he called it King, it slept in a plastic container with air holes at the top

and my protests were nothing down the rattling metal pull-down stairs where he came with the wobbling box in hand, how sad it actually was to see the spider uselessly point his legs in the air as if to sense a threat in this house with a Disney princess quilt and frieze for his six-year-old daughter who stays each Saturday, we don't talk about her, he hides the spiders when she comes around, I am not enough to have them hidden for, the blanket of my apron is a pouch for King and in the dirt of his kitchen I would like to go home.

We chew processed meat in the grand old hall, my hand on a gilded bannister. Above a musical washboard, they hang like ceramic angels, faces chipped, hands chipped with warts from galvanised steel and other kitchenalia.

My mother folding tumble dryer tubes next to the sleeping baby while detergent wends through her arteria, replicating in the blood and gathering as a bright yellow crud in the historical river, brown toxins shared down the gene pool.

Too young to work, but still changing beds in the early hours for a holiday cottage foaming at the mouth for a future untenable, stealing biscuits from a tin. A lousy future that taunts itself on the end of a string, composting from the inside out like a Halloween pumpkin gone bad. I will ask my mother to push me through the ivory gates. I will raid the box of coupons for an answer. Lost to the coins kept in the Steradent tin. I will steal from my own mother to make myself feel richer, and smoke her old cigarettes to make myself sicker, become impregnated with ideas and resist her own impregnation, cut anything out of me that starts to grow in there.

Up the chimney and towards the field, a stark bright woman in glowering dusk wears blinding white, and like a fish she sheds herself, and in her hand, she holds something small, ungrippable.

# Remedies

Seek god's face in the pustule of a teenage girl
whose wrists smell like table sugar
whose hand you hold
under the green and white striped awning
of the beach cafe. Sand blows into ham sandwiches
while distemper accumulates at sea.
*Green parsley and an excess of vitamins*
we whisper remedies out of habit.
If we are passing through the water
and the water is delivering us from evil
forgiving us our trespasses, as we forgive
the cramping tide and waves
we might eventually enjoy grainy tea
in cardboard containers
and look forward to late at night
her arm stretched across me
pressing into my stomach and counting down
the space between waves
a best friend with green eyes
as shallow as a harbour pool.

## Tower of Masks

Chisel at a
bout of stone
head of hair
picked from
rock, incorruptible
in among
the citizenry
she is framed
cherubic against glass
and people congregate
like eyes on
the end of a stalk
picked out
from the crowd
a reclining stone
the woman
is fuller with
her captured rock
inside the modulating
curve, the dish
of her hip
puckered as
flesh is, orbed
and facing up

~

Girl in the shadows
still and marble
the preferred stone.

Girl with a full old
and baroque heart
remains stationary.
Girl with pain in the shins
deep muscle burning
delinquent, mineral eyes
nothing like anything
but a tower of lips
now I am obsessed.
Blue expression of trees
I see in them, faces
stacked on faces

~

Kneeling, hard limestone
the tower of masks
wears concern
and surveillance
in tribute and desire
they cannot
touch themselves
anxiety around
self-promotion
the worthless old
sits in the darkness.
To lay down
and be lovestruck
out of nowhere
and then to be
carved in stone
and to never take
your arms away
from your face

to never take
your arms to
someone's face
that is a gift.
Indecent, the length
of the shadow
of the aqueduct
so dark it nightly
turns the forest blue

# Prairie Burning

There is a man
who circles the perimeter
with a baby in his arms
unmoving.
Locusts burn
with the silhouettes
of saints at dusk.
Saints are in the cloud.
We are in a dry storm.
The man extends his circles
pulling the baby through
the cactus scrub.
Look at his melting trainers
in the heat
they aren't what he asked for.
There are black leather skids
on the dry-stone wall.
People in black cloaks run
out of the corner of your eye.
A hog turns on a spit.
The prairie is a terrarium for the blaze
but the edge is dry of fire.
It is the height of one season,
bushes burn.
A burnt five-year-old
without eyelids
turns quick cartwheels
through the heat wave
under the big pale sky,
black and blue.

# The Slim Man

A landscape unpainted:
a cold stream of lean black weeds
leading towards a stile
and a field tilting up.
Trees turn to veins against marbly sky
in the half hour before night.

During a certain moon
children are said to have seen
a slim man walking over the field
in a low mist, towards the stile,
leading a girl
in pale blue pinstripes
into the glowing pinstripe forest beyond.

Sometimes he will stop and lean down,
and scrape the earth,
then earth and touch are knotted
for they are both cold.
No one is scared of him,
more of the thick-dark brook, drowned roots
and full night, the pitiful rabbits'
eyes yellow on the hillside.

# Multiflora

Was held stationary on the aqueduct
near the snakeskin hanging from the bridge
thrown up by kids. And on the other side of the ridge
a collision of wasps from somewhere in the growth.
Swimming upstream, insects parch my body.

The day is an oven. I float outwards
in a concentric circle. I will know the pattern of your knee.
I sit by the river and envisage our children.
My ankles give way to other thoughts,
thoughts about stealing, objectify me.

She emerges, caught
in a decision
makes her way upwards
in an initial period of
waiting. She wears
suffering on her head
like sugar on a cake.
Time isn't real.
What weather outside?
Worms of mould
in the fruit. Spools
of dirt in the grooves
of the hair. Half-light,
full light, one beacon
pierces the same time
as the sun rises, and
shows up sweet scum
on the water's surface
dappled like albumen.
I rescue a hazy insect,
she watches and knows
I have secrets.
I fall backwards into
the fiume, wearing a
chalk coat, and a heart-skip.
What will save me.
I tell her I love them all,
but she can't tell me hers.

Landscape for a Dead Woman

*To be beautiful*
*and powerful enough*
*for someone*
*to want to break me*

                *up*

*into syndicated ripples.*

*Later I'll try*
*to rise from these dead.*

laid out on
a shrine

a bloodletting woman
take her to

the sea
fog stuffed

where mayhem
in the slew

of interlocking
waters clarifies

into a vision; a handprint
becomes colloidal

and then she's gone

this is what happens
when a woman dies

the landscape
unlocks from its planning

we are reluctant tenants
no one else lives here

we farmed all the grief

murder is a kind of sorcery
who cursed us?

Can we blame the alignment
of inexplicable circumstances

or was it my fault?
I ask as I'm pushed back into the dark

my mouth a spell of light
*what's going on out there*

the sinking house and the land
are to be consumed

and the sea will obfuscate the shore as she has
obfuscate our lives

murder is
future embarrassment

mother and sister, qualities
calcify in the density of bones

where is she

when she's not with me?
Not back in the old stone kitchen

prone on a cold wood floor
when the water's grey and tactile
I could lift it up like a blanket

and find her hiding underneath
crouched down like a joke

I didn't earn any adulthood
I had it thrust upon me

she visited once
and told me

men have the upper hand
unbanded her chest

to reveal rows of wounds
delivered concomitantly

my vision
is scalded and empty

sweet, insignificant
chatter in the distance

a bad husband loitering
in the kitchen of my mind: damp

he lives in shadow
damp, I cannot place his face

was she alive

when she lived? Did she wear
hooves on her feet?

Did he mistake her for an animal
when he let blood for the night?

She is embedded in the walls
and emerges from the walls

our memories need flushing
like a cistern blocked with blood

I bundle my sister
up in the cloth

deliver her to the
orphanage

where she will be safer away
from her murderous family

where they murder
each other in kitchens

great screaming

certain areas of council do nothing
I thought I saw her

and followed her through the streets
it wasn't her of course

I would have done more than that
I would have brought her back to life

colossal guilt

the size of buses end to end
the size of blue whales spilling from wounds

a picture book of primary colours
featuring increments of size

mean I imagine wounds
not celebratory hands

that touch the children's cake
we keep it from them

my sister in the mist
tugging bones

where the grass dies
murder is a flood

has she gone into liquidation?
When the ice melts will she be there

with a plague
to give to everyone

she has dissolved
an egg in acid

I sit by the lake
with a rod

to wait for her
to come out of the water

and a novelty postcard arrives
from wherever she is

ghosts war in my head
cryptic and mildew

counting all the dead women
putting them in a document

burn all documents
rescue the women

pulling their hair out
she told the operator

she couldn't breathe
and out to sea, blue breath

a blue ghost on the doorstep
but it's not her

she is wholly gone
birds hang like visual disturbance

flick monstrously from side to side
bad pile of sand

no end and no beginning
water laps at my feet

## Apostles Burning

I was one burnt daughter
in a genealogy.
Stepped into the oil
spill like a siren
emerged dyed black
backed with the wings
of a tanker's logo
jangling stranded
in the outer ocean
holding a child
looking for the perfect
swell. Fires edging closer
like dinghies on water.
Apostles hot and orange,
citrus milk I can feed her.

# Banshee

He'll sit by the window
at an innocent date
with wandering hands
over a port-green stool.
There's the kitchen
where she was murdered
where she was delivered
into a weapon with force
like a small model forester
axing up plastic logs
in a red wooden clock
murdered by a man
the sanctity of communion
she was never alone
the heavy smell of blood
misted up past the crockery
and the murdered girls before her
gathered up in plain cotton
the scores of her limbs
and the nub of her treatment
her hair was a clotted
pattern of wallpaper
like a tapestry of rabbits
and they left with her body
but do not forgive
so easily as that.
Tonight she laughs walking
towards his dark house
her head's a dun lantern
with split ends uplifted

her hands are barbed knots
to take it back
for she's fury with a shell
and she's petty.
The old boundary walls
where she leaned in the summer
swaying in her peripherals.
She dons now a grey sheet
the dusk colour of bonbons
to seem more like a haunting
light pools through the mock-glass
and the door she approaches
the red door approaches

The sea flames
an undercurrent.

A girl, strange beliefs
present in the water

turns through plastic
holds to the drift

bathing in the black and
emergent pond.

Lungless, she
caves with the weight

see the water's charge
boil simultaneously

as the girls float up
to the billowing ceiling.